WHIPPIN DEBT'S ASS!

BUDGET, SAVE, INVEST, AND LIVE.

STENELL MYERS

www.stenellthemoneytherapist.com

WHIPPIN DEBT'S ASS!

BUDGET, SAVE, INVEST, AND LIVE.

Whippin Debt's Ass is an easy quick read with details on how my husband Tony and I got out of debt. This book can help only if you are ready to take the steps to make a lifelong commitment to yourself. Applying these steps and really wanting to see the results in your finances starts with you. I decided if I can do this and it works for me and my family, I can share this with the world to help others. The chapters are titled as evidence-based because the steps I took to get out of debt are goal-oriented and are grounded in tangible outcomes. The conclusion of each chapter shares a money tip, summarizing key points to think about and apply, so you too can whip debt's ass.

WHIPPIN DEBT'S ASS - "Budget, Save, Invest, and Live"

DEDICATION AND ACKNOWLEDGEMENTS

This book is dedicated to married couples, single men and woman, single moms and dads, high school, and college students. In essence, anyone who is tired of allowing debt to control their emotions and their life; for everyone who is ready to change their negative financial situation to a positive one, permanently. I am going to deliver all of me and be unapologetic of who I am. There are so many of you drowning in your finances, with no plan, running in circles just like I was. My goal is to reach the emotional you. I want you to feel the pain I endured as if it was your own so you can say,

"I am tired and ready to **WHIP THIS DEBT'S ASS!**"

I am eternally grateful to my mom. I thank you for giving me life and being the strong, single mother that provided for me and my brothers. I love everything about you from your strong personality to your giving heart. Thank you for raising me to be strong, independent, and to never be afraid to speak my truth, even when it was difficult. I do all that I do because I watched you do whatever was necessary to provide for us. You're the best.

To my husband Tony, you always support me and rarely say no. Thank you for championing all my projects, visions, and new business ventures and helping out the men from a male's perspective combining finances in the chapter It's Better to Whip Debt Together Than Separate. Even when you do not understand why I do so much, you allow me to be me.

To my children, Zaquell, Ryann, Unique, and Genesis, you are the reason I grind and work hard. I love you all, as you are all unique in your own way. As I always say, my prayer for each of you is to fly like a bird and do you. Life is too short, and you must answer God's call.

A very special thank you to John Cummutta for introducing me to your Transforming Debt into Wealth (TDIW) System 15 years ago. Although I struggled for years to dedicate myself to your technique, your teaching was always in the back of my mind. In fact, I still have your green large working TDIW System on the side of my bed as a quick reference to keep me on track.

Dave Ramsey, I thank you for your honesty and technique of teaching how to stay out of debt. At the time when I was introduced to you via the internet, I was more mature and in a better financial situation. This enabled me to follow your steps, lead two financial Peace University groups and become certified through your master trainer course to help others with money. The combination of both John Cummutta and Dave Ramsey has paved the way for me and so many others to take control of their finances.

None of this would have been possible without my cousin, Ebonie. No matter how far we are, your encouraging words make me leap and do everything God called me to do. Every time we have our yearly four-hour conversations, it turns into a project for me. I believe God speaks through you to send me messages. That is why after we talk, my obedience takes over and a new project is created. Thank you for telling me to be my own voice and create my own path. Your encouraging words make me feel like I can take over the world.

And finally, to Tamika Chester, I always say God finds the ram in the bush when you need it. Thank you for being my ram and helping me when I did not know I needed help. Thank you for knowing before I knew that I was not walking in my truth. Thank you for being real; you are a true friend.

$EVIDENCE-BASED CHAPTERS$

ONE

THE INTRODUCTION TO WHIPPIN DEBT'S ASS

Has something or someone ever made you feel anger, frustration, and rage that you wanted nothing other than to put your hands on them? This is what debt did to me. I was not getting anywhere. Just living check to check with no budget, no plan, and no financial future.

I decided to share my experiences and write Whippin Debt's Ass in 2018 after paying off $50,000 in debt in one year and educating my friends and church family how to do the same.

It's now 2022. COVID-19, purchasing my dream home in Florida, and moving my mother in with me put a halt to getting this book published and released.

You are about to read my financial perspective on finances and the steps I took to not only get and stay out of debt but help others do the same. Are you ready to apply the tools I am sharing with you so you can whip debt's ass budget, save, invest, and live?

I HAD A DREAM, AND YOU ARE READING THE OUTCOME

We are executives of our lives and the choices we make. We

choose to do what we want related to our life and our finances. The money we have has no power. We hold the power. We make our own choices, and we write our own book. We will no longer make excuses about money we do not have and instead, learn to be good stewards with the money we do have.

STENELL THE MONEY THERAPIST

TWO

$HUMBLE BEGINNING$$

I am a mental health therapist that was called to help people across many disciplines through education initiatives, social-emotional training, non-profit literacy, and of course, through money management. I cast a wide net and reach not only to entrepreneurs looking to start their own business but to those with developmental disabilities and mental illness as well.

I let my passion and profession intertwine as I found myself teaching and talking about how to handle and manage money with a plan instead of money managing me without a plan. In my senior year of high school, I was accepted to Norfolk State University and was eager to join two of my best friends there. Instead, at the age of 18, I got pregnant with my son.

Although I graduated high school, my dream to attend a four-year college was crushed. Six years later, I had my first baby girl. Six years after that, I was married and had my second baby girl.

Here I was, having a child every six years with different

men. Each time I thought I was in love. I had no direction on handling my personal life, had no clue how to handle money, nor did I know how to run a business. My personal and financial lives were in communal chaos.

For three years, I taught a total of seven different psychology courses as an adjunct professor at Camden County College and Drexel University. I always had a passion for saving money and purchasing rental homes as investment opportunities. I read countless books about real estate investments and money. I would watch infomercials and purchase DVDs and audio tapes regarding how to build wealth with real estate investments. Basically, I ordered anything that would teach me how to increase my net worth. I recall reading as many articles as I could from Essence magazine related to money and relationships to educate myself.

During my time as an adjunct professor, I constantly found myself making the effort to teach my adult college students about money and real estate investments. Ironically, this was when I was receiving unemployment, teaching three classes, and did not own any businesses. At this time, my current business ventures were not even in the pre-planning stages, but I had this unexplained passion that would constantly jump out of me regarding money and business. Like any passion, I would share it with anyone that would listen. When I talk about starting a business or a project, it is never just talk. The conversation always evolves into a real-life adventure.

In order to act upon my passion, I knew I had to learn how to oversee my money. As my non-profit business dreams grew into reality, I started making more money than I ever had before. Then I hit rock bottom. I was treating my business like my own personal ATM.

I knew I had to learn how to oversee my finances.

I had never seen so much money in a month before, and three things were certain: I had no plan, no plan, and no plan. This is when I came to learn that the saying "when you make money, you get stupid" is absolutely true. I drained money from my business for three years. I cannot tell you how much money I wasted through impulsive spending. I would make purchases for whatever I wanted, whenever I wanted, and I had no contingency plan. I did not have a personal or business emergency fund. My tax account balance was always zero. I just was dumb; there is no other way to say it.

My personal debt consisted of two car loans and four credit cards. I was charging absolutely everything on my credit card, even the pavers for my backyard. There was no concept of planning and saving for what I wanted. As the money came in I spent it. My spending was downright ridiculous. Here I was, a boss, the chief executive officer of two agencies with over 20 employees, a landlord managing a profitable duplex; yet I was doing everything wrong financially. I was watching all my hard work go to waste. I got emotionally sick when I saw the end of the year statement from my for-profit business.

At this point, I'd had enough. I decided that instead of managing everybody else, it was time I started managing myself.

THREE

$MY BREAKING POINT$

I was a single mom of three children with a master's degree, working as a therapist supervisor at an outpatient mental health agency; yet I was still struggling to keep up with the gas and electric bill and put food on the table. I would constantly find myself asking my nieces if they could spare their Electronic Benefit Transfer (EBT) card so I could get food at the beginning of the month.

Everyone who understands the struggle will understand this calculation: $150 for $300. This would help me get food for the month and would give my niece extra money to pay a bill or put toward the rent. That was a very difficult time in my life. Although I am in a different place today, I would still use that bad boy if my nieces needed extra money.

This was my monthly money struggle each year, until tax return time. You see, in my culture, the income tax check is like the second coming of Christmas. January 2nd rolls around, and you are already planning to go on vacation, buy furniture, buy clothes, make a down payment for a car, and all other non-essential spending you can do with this surplus income.

Year after year, I found myself using my precious tax return check to dig myself further into debt. I was paying all or most of my credit card debt and car loans two or three months in advance, but then booking an all-inclusive vacation that cost over $2,000. Of course, this $2,000 does not include the flight, fly vacation clothes (that no one cares about), and other travel expenses such as a rental car.

Don't forget the daily airport parking, food (if it is not an all-inclusive package) and spending money for excursions. That $2,000 just turned into a quick $3,500. It was a vicious cycle, and Tony and I did this for eight years of our marriage. At the end of each summer, we found ourselves back in credit card debt.

The end of each vacation symbolized the end of our clean credit history because ultimately, we were back making monthly payments to creditors. All because vacations and other activities were a priority instead of chipping away at our debt. We constantly found ourselves paying, charging, paying, and charging with no end in sight.

One day, I said to myself, "I can't do this anymore!" The cycle of paying, charging, paying, and charging created debt in both my personal and business endeavors. I was drowning, and my debt was choking me. I felt as though I could not breathe, and I was angry all the time. I was a complete mess for a little over a week. I was yelling at my husband and at my kids. I was coming home exhausted only to have to cook and clean, until one day, I just snapped and had a severe meltdown.

I went to Tony and told him that I was ready to give it all up. With over 20 employees and two businesses relying on me, there was a tremendous weight on my shoulders to run the businesses and to make sure I could afford payroll.

All of this, and we couldn't even get our personal finances in order. I told myself that if I didn't find out how to strategically finance my business and manage my personal finances, I was done.

And I meant it. I scared myself. I knew if I did not turn this around, I was in jeopardy of ruining everything I worked so hard for and, more importantly, I was endangering what God graced me to do, which was to help others. I had hit rock bottom in my thoughts and my emotions. I was not happy, and the only people that knew were my family; my staff had no clue.

That is what really motivated me to change. My staff relied on a strong, courageous leader, and here I was, ready to give it all up. That pressure made me wash my face and pull it together. I had too many people trusting in me. I had to turn what I was feeling around because if I did not, I would not be able to share my testimony.

Debt is real, and it can suffocate your thoughts, emotions, and keep you awake at night. You can feel so low that the only solution you may come up with is to get into more debt to pay off your current debt. Or you may choose to ignore it because the consumption of the debt is too much. My truth is your truth. Maybe not in this form, but I know you can relate to my story, my pain, and my passion.

Your past decisions are controlling your future decisions.

This is not how things should be. If you are tired of waking up early every day to go to work just to find yourself paying bills every 30 days as if your job is to pay bills, then do what I did. Whip debt's ass and move on to live the good life God created you to live. You may be saying, "How in the world is Stenell using Ass and God in the same sentence?" Listen, I sincerely love God and talk about him throughout this book, my videos, and clients' consultations.

I did whip debt's ass, and I have no words to use other than my own. I do not sugarcoat. I do not manipulate my truth to satisfy anyone else's feelings, nor do I try to make anyone feel comfortable. In fact, I want you to feel what I felt. I want you to feel so uncomfortable that you do something immediately.

The number one lesson you will learn from this money therapist is to know your truth, speak your truth, and live your truth. If you are not engaging in these three areas of not just money, but your own personal wellness, then you will not be able to truly satisfy you. In the words of Russel Simmons, "it is time to do you," because you are important to you.

We all are placed on this earth to help people in whatever capacity God intended. This is the main reason for our existence. I know my "why." My "why" is to help you get out of debt, formulate a weekly, biweekly, or monthly budget, pull that business out of you, help you build your faith, and set attainable and measurable goals. You can only do these things with a plan. It is time to put the "I can't," "I don't know how," "It will always be like this," and the "I don't care anymore" out of your soul. It is time to do what God intended for you to do, and that is, whip this debt's ass like you never whipped anything before!

MONEY TIP:

Let your breaking point be your starting point. Create detailed financial goals and execute them with attainable outcomes. If your mental state is not in order and your mind is cluttered, you will not have your finances in order.

FOUR

$IT IS BETTER TO WHIP DEBT TOGETHER THAN SEPARATE$

This year, Tony and I will celebrate our tenth anniversary. We have a blended family of six children, which means we deal with many different personalities that are not always biologically like our own. Yes, it has been difficult, but I am glad we both made a commitment to make our family work, much like our finances. In the beginning, our finances were a mess because we both had no real concept of planning and budgeting our money as a couple.

Tony worked his steady career as a correctional officer, and I worked in the field of mental health. Financially, we thought we were doing everything right because we survived before we met each other. The week we were married, we both granted each other access to our bank accounts, but we did not combine them. Our first attempt to manage our money as a married couple was horrible.

It was not that there was not enough money, it was that we both came into the marriage with debt, so now everything was doubled. This meant double the car payments, double the credit cards and double the childcare costs. I also brought in student loans, and we still had to pay the mortgage. Tony put me in charge of paying the bills as long as he had money in his pocket for lunch, bowling, and spending.

Because of this, Tony viewed any financial hiccups as my fault instead of the fault of our decision-making. Because of the separation of bank accounts, the struggle with money began to tear our marriage apart. To be honest, we almost did not make it through our first year. Tony was a bachelor who was used to spending his money on whatever and whoever he chose, and I was a single mom of three just trying to get by. It has only been two years since we combined our bank accounts.

The combination of understanding how to budget and how to execute a budget has made a huge positive impact in our marriage, so here we stand 10 years later. Now Tony and I teach couples about the importance of getting on board with the direction of their finances.

Ten years ago, I would never have thought we would be at a place where he agreed to openly talk about money, let alone to help other couples come up with a financial plan to strengthen their marriages. When I first set out to tackle our debt, I talked to Tony about it. He was not on board and did not want to get rid of his credit cards because they were a part of his money habit. Outwardly, he was not interested in helping me with the budget as long as he got his spending money.

But if something went wrong with our accounts, he would blame me. Our money was not separate, but our mindsets were. We both had independent ideas about what we would do with our money once we got paid. Quite frankly, I was glad that he did not control his income because it made it easier for me to prove to him that I was doing right by his paycheck. This also allowed him to start listening as he saw the results. To get him to start listening, I had to change my communication style from aggressive to assertive.

I began speaking in a soft tone, which went against all my basic instincts, and Tony opened up to my new approach. It was not easy and took Tony four months to come around.

According to a survey from SunTrust Bank reported on CNBC, finances are the leading cause of stress in relationships for couples aged 44 to 55.

As Tony and I counseled couples through financial stability, we learned why this is true. In our class, we often heard couples say that they kept their money separate for many reasons, the main reason being trust.

We learned that one or both individuals in the relationship did not trust the other with handling their money. I myself had trust issues. However, like with any area of trust, ignoring the core of the problem will always cause the problem to resurface, unresolved.

Of course, there are situations where couples have no choice but to keep their money separate. If one spouse is engaged in an addictive behavior or is irresponsible with money, the responsible spouse must govern the finances to keep a roof over their heads.

There are many different dysfunctions that may cause money in a relationship to be separate. If this is the case, I suggest that you and your spouse seek marriage counseling to help you with your issues.

This will put you both on a path to resolve dysfunction and establish trust as the basis of a plan that will help you have success with your marriage and your finances. It is very important to work together on your finances because you are married. As one couple, there should be an understanding that no matter how much money either spouse brings in, you are aware and budgeting your finances together.

Now, ladies and gentlemen, I must break down this topic from a male and female perspective so you each understand your roles. Wives, I am going to try and help you get your husband on board. Husbands, Tony is going to share his knowledge to help you through and stay true to the process.

You can both thank me later when you listen or watch my podcast at www.stenellthemoneytherapist.com/podcast

WIVES

The most beneficial advice I can give is for you to be true to the process and be consistent. If you truly want to change your finances and see a true change in your husband, you must change first. This means you must learn and understand your money communication style and change what isn't working.

Your new communication style should be assertive yet soft-spoken. In the next chapter, I will go into greater depth about communication style and money habits. The important thing to remember is that you are now leading by example and imparting that you are serious.

This means you are consistently budgeting all income. If your husband is not on board initially, don't panic. Remain calm and continue to budget what you have control over while asking for his input and showing him how you need him to be on board. This also means you are not spending money frivolously.

You are not purchasing shoes, clothes, purses, or going out doing you. Instead, you have a detailed plan to pay the bills you normally pay while walking your husband through the process. You are quietly taking charge and showing your maturity as the entrepreneur of your finances.

If you do not do this consistently, then your husband won't buy in, and he will not get on board. When he does start to concede to the process, award him with a kiss, a massage, or whatever you reward him with, so you stay the course together. You must do this for yourself, your children, and God.

God created you to be a helpmate to your husband, not his opponent. Don't argue and don't raise your voice. Just change the game and show your husband not only that you know how to whip debt's ass but that you both can whip debt's ass together.

HUSBANDS

Hi ladies and fellas, this is Tony. Whippin debt's ass was a process for me. Like my wife stated earlier, I was not on board. Primarily, I had concerns about having enough money to buy things for my daughter that did not live with us.

At the time, my mind told me that not having a credit card meant I would not have any money. As a father, I did not want my daughter to want for anything. I also never said no to any of her wants, as most fathers do.

I was faced with the fear of disappointing my child, but I also understood that my marital money situation was dire and needed to change.

By executing her money plan, Stenell was able to pay off one of our credit cards. This made me realize that if she could do that by herself, then together we could really conquer our debt.

Combining her business profits and my willingness to work overtime, we successfully got rid of **$50,000** worth of credit cards and car loan debt in one year. I now understand that budgeting must be a way of life.

Like Benjamin Franklin said, *"If you fail to plan, you are planning to fail."*

Successful budgeting involves executing a plan with your spouse. It involves two minds coming together with one common goal: to whip debt's ass!

MONEY TIP:

If you are married with combined bank accounts, it is important to outline each and every budget together using the spreadsheet at www.stenellthemoneytherpist.com.
This way, you both are on the same page and can agree on what is important for the week or month, depending on how you are budgeting. If you are not married, enlist a reliable friend or partner, so you can work together but separately to support each other.

Working together in any capacity encourages unity.

FIVE

$COMMUNICATION STYLE AND MONEY HABITS$

Over the course of my experience with youth social-emotional programs, I worked with elementary and secondary students to teach them how to effectively communicate their thoughts, help them understand how to appropriately engage with their peers and build healthy relationships.

Recently, while I was teaching a finance group, I began to realize that there is a strong correlation between our style of communication and how we handle our finances. Listening to each person express their experience regarding finances and relationships made me understand the power of communication in healthy relationships.

My days of teaching psychology and life skills came flooding back to me. My background as a counselor in the fields of mental health, relationships and finances, and experience as a psychology instructor made me wonder how money and psychology were linked.

The psychology behind our monetary decisions is the key to understanding so many variables regarding how we properly or improperly handle our finances.

Without understanding the link between money and psychology, so many questions can go unanswered. Why do certain people become wealthy, and others do not?

How do wealthy celebrities squander their fortunes in just a few years?

Why does one person in a relationship mishandle money and the other is responsible with money?

Why are some people able to save money and others are financially irresponsible by spending all the money they earn without saving?

Yes, our upbringing and culture are key to how we process our thoughts when it comes to our finances.

However, the way we exchange information and convey our feelings and ideas to others is intrinsically linked to the way we spend our money.

As I stated in the previous chapter, using an assertive communication style is the biggest key to a healthy relationship with money. The lesson I am about to discuss may not be comfortable for you.

What follows will help you to identify the type of communication style you engage in, and depending on your style, require you to make improvements and adjustments on how you communicate with others as well as how you handle your money.

You may find that you use multiple styles of communication in different environments such as at work and at home or among different groups of colleagues.

It is important to be aware of your communication style(s) and work to improve your communication skills, so you can have better relationships, including relationships with money. Outlined below are the basic tenets of four central communication styles: *passive, aggressive, passive aggressive, and assertive.*

Illustrated below are four examples of the communication style of using the same scenario to help you identify your style.

PASSIVE COMMUNICATION is an avoidance of one's own feelings and opinions. You fail to express your point of view or assert yourself out of either apathy or fear. You have explosive outbursts after reaching your tolerance threshold. Oftentimes, repressing your true feelings results in you not maturing in needed areas.

EXAMPLE OF PASSIVE COMMUNICATION: You do not understand what is going on with your finances and genuinely, do not want to be the overseer of them. When the time comes to go over the finances with your spouse or accountability partner, you see inconstancies and may have an idea to help in this area, but you do not speak up and go along with the current plan although you do not agree.

You find yourself saying things like, "I'm fine with whatever you want to do."

PASSIVE COMMUNICATION AND MONEY.

You may feel like you have no control over your money. You

stay away as much as possible from overseeing your household bills and leave that to your spouse or partner. If you are single, you do what you can and may ignore creditors, which results in poor credit. Finances make you feel intimidated.

You have no order.

You do not pay your bills on time.

You easily get anxious and sometimes fail to ask creditors questions because of this anxiety.

Ultimately, you ignore the issue, and nothing is resolved as the problem gets worse.

AGGRESSIVE COMMUNICATION is the opposite of passive communication. This communication style is marked by being heavily critical of others, blaming, dominating, lack of impulse control, rudeness, demanding, and exhibiting low tolerance of ideas different from your own.

EXAMPLE OF AGGRESSIVE COMMUNICATION: Because you do not know what is going on with the finances, you lose your cool and begin to blame and make others feel responsible for your lack of knowing or understanding. If the finances are not in order, it is the fault of the other person and none of your own.

You find yourself saying things like, "It is all your fault that we are in this mess."

AGGRESSIVE COMMUNICATION AND MONEY.

You do not think prior to spending. You may give hasty thought before making a purchase, but your aggressive personality leads to overindulgence and gives no regard to responsibility.

You make impulsive purchases that you did not budget for and therefore, have developed a work hard, play hard mindset. Your retort to creditors is often "when I get the money, you will get the money."

All the while, you continue to make unbudgeted purchases.

Your wants supersede your needs.

You spend money while rationalizing your purchases in your head without a detailed plan.

To you, it makes sense to go on a vacation that you did not budget for, even if it means maxing out your credit cards or spending your rent or mortgage money because of your aggressive nature.

PASSIVE AGGRESSIVE COMMUNICATION is when you appear docile and cool on the surface while accepting uncomfortable situations because you struggle with confrontation and straightforwardness.

This unease turns into anger manifesting as resentment. You feel powerless and incapable of confronting or handling a situation and express your frustration through a delicate tone.

EXAMPLE OF PASSIVE AGGRESSIVE COMMUNICATION: When it is time to go over the finances with your spouse or accountability partner, you do enough to get him or her off your back. Or you avoid financial conversations altogether by saying you will get to it, knowing in the back of your mind that you really do not care and are going to continue paying or avoiding the bills the way you see fit.

You find yourself saying things like, "Sure, we can handle this your way, but I wouldn't be surprised if it doesn't work."

PASSIVE AGGRESSIVE COMMUNICATION AND MONEY.

You're having an inner conflict with yourself and your financial choices. You often say you will organize your bills and begin to plan and pay your debt. You know what actions you must take to get on track with your finances, but you never take them.

You avoid your bill collectors and become angry with them instead of facing the situation and working out a plan. Meanwhile, your tone is settled and calm, and you may outwardly appear to be compliant. In reality, you are telling yourself you are not paying anything and continue this process, so your situation does not resolve or get better.

Because this area is very sensitive, you do not handle your finances in a responsible manner and will spend your money on other things you deem important. You spend money on a vacation or the purchase of a car without finding a solution or owning your responsibility to get your debt paid.

ASSERTIVE COMMUNICATION is an awareness of your emotions that includes an expressed value of yourself and your time as well as an awareness of other peoples' feelings. You are appropriate in expressing your needs and wants and possess good listening skills. As problems arise, they are addressed, which allows maturity to manifest.

EXAMPLE OF ASSERTIVE COMMUNICATION: When it is time to go over the finances, you have a detailed weekly, biweekly, or monthly budget. All budgeted income is linked to paying bills with concrete plans of what will happen with any surplus of money, and you and your spouse or accountability partner are on the same page with a plan.

If either person has any input, it is respectfully discussed ending with a comprise or execution of the plan.

You find yourself saying things like, "We are equally responsible for handling our money, and we are going to do it the right way, together."

ASSERTIVE COMMUNICATION AND MONEY.

You make rational purchasing decisions and save for larger purchases. You develop financial goals that are related to meeting your needs while working from a detailed financial plan. You learn through trial and error and confront yourself when you are about to make an unplanned and irrational purchasing decision.

You make financial improvements in needed areas and have confidence in how you control your finances.

You budget for high-priced items you want instead of making impulsive purchases. When your friends or family ask to borrow money, you tell them your truth.

You do not lie or make excuses, rather you educate them about financial planning so they can learn to be independent.

MONEY TIP:

Keep a journal and write down your current style of communication. Identify the financial area or areas in which you struggle to be assertive. Chart the action steps you will take to help you in that area. Repeat this process for each area you need to address. This takes time, but you must be honest with yourself and speak your truth.

Doing this will help you make better choices when it comes to how you spend your money. If you stay the course, you will see a change in your communication style with money while working toward being assertive with your finances.

You will also see a change as you become more assertive in your personal relationships.

SIX

$OWNING MY NO'$$

It was October 2017 when I said no to debt. I decided that we were going to do something different with our finances that would change our lives. Our youngest girls were both juniors in high school and were gearing up to graduate the following year.

I used my newfound passion for planning to project all the infinite debt that comes along with high school graduates such as senior trip, senior pictures, prom, and prom weekend. But then there was college to consider.

Staring into the face of multiple college tuitions, we realized that we had very little in the way of a financial plan.

The saving grace was that our son received a full track scholarship in 2012.

Because of this, we did not feel the pain of not having a college financial plan until our girls were about to graduate in the same year.

We already decided that we were going to say no to college loans, so ourselves and our children were not in debt. We needed a game plan quick. We had savings but nothing like a long-term birth to college savings account, which would have helped us tremendously.

Regardless, I had to learn the word "no" quickly and made sure that everyone around me understood my definition of "no," which meant "hell no."

Luckily, I've never had a problem saying what I mean.

I've always seen my communication style to be assertive mixed with some aggression.

So naturally, I was down for saying no to anyone and anything, especially my kids.

I knew that if Tony and I stuck to saying no, we would conquer this debt. When we decided to take this journey to be debt free, it was not hard to be assertive and tell people we were working on a financial plan that would help us to get out of debt.

Tony and I had to make smart decisions when choosing how to spend our free time (and money) and making purchases that were not in our budget. I cannot count how many times we had to say "no" to things and people.

Oftentimes, we could not go out with friends because it was not in the budget. "It is not in our budget" became our motto.

Surprisingly, Tony would even come home and tell me how he would say "it is not in our budget" to his co-workers.

By doing this, we felt empowered to stay on track, managing our debt and budget. This made our marriage more unified, knowing we had a plan. It also began to alleviate the stress of debt and not having a plan.

By now, you may be asking yourself how you can make "it

is not in our budget" your motto too.

In order to illustrate how, I made a list of the no's we used and a few good examples so you can practice. Remember that saying "no" is empowering because you are in control of you.

In these situations, **"no"** must be your go to word:

> » NO, I can't go out to dinner, unless you are buying.
> » Car dealer, do you take cash? You only finance or lease? NO thank you. I only pay with cash.
> » NO Visa, Mastercard, and Discover; I don't need to borrow money. I can do this on my own.
> » NO vacation for me, unless it's local.
> » NO, I must decline attending your wedding. I cannot buy you a gift or give you money.
> » NO, I cannot go to the movies, sorry. I will wait for it to come out on the Fire Stick.
> » It's your birthday? NO, I can't buy you a gift. Maybe when I get out of debt though.
> » You said all-you-can-eat crabs? My favorite. I will budget for crab legs when I go grocery shopping. I will put them in an aluminum pan, add Old Bay, corn, and potatoes. In my mind, I am out eating with you at Joe's Crab Shack. NO, I cannot go to all-you-can-eat crab night.

I know I am dramatic, but I really said most of these things, and it worked. Think about it, saying yes to all those things leaves you in the same cycle: **BROKE.** Resolving to end the cycle and rearranging all "yes" habits to "no" habits is the only way out. To do this, you must decide what was important to your family and be realistic about your current situation.

Tony and I understood that our biggest sacrifice and firmest "no" would have to be to ourselves.

We love to go on vacations; mini weekend getaways, long getaways, any getaway as long as we were getting away.

But we weren't being realistic about our current debt. We calculated that our vacation spending ate up a large percentage of our income.

Oftentimes, we were still paying off debt that included vacations from the previous year while planning for new vacations. It took us one year to pay off roughly **$50,000** in debt, which included four credit cards, and two car notes.

Each month, we were paying a total of $1,500 to bill collectors and creditors. All of that money, and we were just paying off debt, not putting food on the table or paying the mortgage

For these reasons, it only made sense to cut out vacations all together. Tony and I agreed that while we were paying off debt, we would cut up our credit cards and cancel them, enabling us to stay out of debt permanently.

This meant we now had to learn to pay with cash for everything, even cars. Never again would we have a car loan, because monthly car payments were draining our future retirement investments.

Instead of shelling out $300 to $530 a month in car payments, we invested that money in our Individual Retirement Account (IRA).

All cultures, people, and situations are different. What worked for me may not work for you, but the word "no" is universal.

If you learn to not only say "no" but really take action, you will see the difference in your situation.

Yes, ma'ams don't get far in life.

It is those who stand up and make a change that succeed. By being true to your "no" with a plan and a budget, you too will succeed.

MONEY TIP:

Saying no can be difficult and may cause anxiety because this is new, and you are not used to being in control. Each time you say no to your kids, your friends, or even yourself when it comes to your finances, you are on the path of maturation. On a calendar, your phone, or wherever you take notes, write down the details of each time you say no regarding spending money. Do this for 60 days. At the end of each month, take an inventory and review how many days you said no. As the 60-day mark approaches, you should see an improvement. Continue this process of review and reflection until you have turned all your "yes" habits into "no" habits.

SEVEN

$ANOTHER PAYCHECK$

The three years it took to launch my businesses were very difficult likely because I founded a for-profit and non-profit agency simultaneously, not for lack of preparation.

My undergraduate grant writing classes and doctorate courses in multidisciplinary leadership made me aware of the skillsets required to run an organization. In my doctorate courses is where I found my niche.

Everything I am doing today as an entrepreneur and businesswoman stems from my multidisciplinary studies. It was well worth the five years of hard work and internships. I am who I am today because I have applied what I learned in college to run my companies.

By the way, I decided not to write my dissertation at the completion of my doctoral program. So, I am a Ph.D. ABD (All But Dissertation) and proud of it.

But that is another conversation for another time.

With both agencies up and running, I was receiving a paycheck from the non-profit, but not the for-profit. I was doing well paying my bills and my monthly debt from the combination of other income.

Still, I could not afford to pay myself from the for-profit. I would withdraw money from time to time, but I thought that is what you were supposed to do as a business owner of a for-profit.

I had no system or organization for my for-profit like I had for my non-profit. I did not start paying myself from the for-profit agency until three years after the business started. I did not pay myself much. I paid myself what I could afford because I placed priority on making sure my staff was paid.

Once the company made more of a profit, I put myself on the payroll. This is the teachable moment for all you entrepreneurs at heart. I had the ability to put myself on my payroll, and I could not believe it. It was an amazing feeling after working for three years.

Even though I had been ready to give up many times, I was finally able to take home a paycheck. I could not tell you what I did with that money for the first year.

I have no clue because I did not give my checks an assignment. One thing was for certain; the more money I made, the more I spent.

Here I was with double the income and nothing tangible to show for it. I did not even have an emergency fund. I was frivolous with this new income when I should have been applying the entire check to our debt instead.

Many times, we get a part-time job to bring in extra income so it can help pay the bills when our primary job is not enough on which to survive. Or maybe you have a job that offers over-time, and that money is applied to help pay the bills.

This chapter is very important because sometimes we are blessed with another source of income, but without a plan we end up missing the blessing behind those resources God provided for us.

The examples in this chapter are meant to show you what extra income is NOT to be used for in order to change the way you look at your money.

The way we see our money has everything to do with how we spend the money, which is why you see people that win millions of dollars in the lottery go broke five years later.

By changing my perception of money, I was able to pay $50,000 in debt within a year.

By building yourself up and altering your relationship with money, you too will see a change.

As a general rule, when you are in debt, extra income should NOT be used for:

» **Vacations;**

» **Purchasing hundred dollars of hair extensions and installation;**

» **Pedicures (Get your toes polished and paint your nails yourself; it is cheaper);**

» **Buying outfits to go out to dinner, parties, and vacation (No one cares what you wear);**

» **Expensive clothes for yourself or your kids;**

» **Expensive sneakers (Michael Jordan is already rich, and he does not need your money);**

» **Electronics for yourself or your kids;**

» **Excursions at your local beach, such as jet skiing or boat rentals.**

These are all ways I misused my money. Of all of these things I was spending my money on, none of them were assisting me with my debt or helping me to build wealth. Once you are out of debt, you can catalogue these wants and manage your spending with a system (more on that later).

To manage my spending, I took each check and applied it to my debt and only my debt.

That meant no movies, going out to dinner, or play money. I had one purpose for my money, and that was to pay off my debt in full.

Here's an example of how to manage your money:

You have a Mastercard with a $4,500 balance.

Your extra paycheck or overtime check is $395.

You send Mastercard the entire $395.

Now your balance is $4,105 ($4,500 - $395 = $4,105).

You send Mastercard your next biweekly paycheck of $395, and it brings your balance to $3,710.

After doing this for five months, your Mastercard is now paid in full.

The more money you send, the faster you can whip down this debt. Apply this concept with any extra income you receive.

MONEY TIP:

Stay true to this process and watch the debt get smaller. You will feel one of two emotions, either happy to see the debt disappearing or upset with yourself as you try to figure out how you got so deep in debt in the first place. Remember that if you stick to applying any extra money to your debt, in time, it will disappear.

EIGHT

$THE DIFFERENT BURNER SYNDROME$

Getting out of debt meant that I had to become my own therapist. I had to look at myself and say, "Listen, Stenell, you beautiful princess, you prayed for what you have, and you are blowing all your hard work on things that you don't even remember buying."

I told myself to get it together.

I had to unlearn my old money management habits and relearn a new way to keep and invest my money because I was ruining my future self.

I began to read as many books as I could and saw a change in my thoughts about money.

I began to think about my future in terms of when and where I wanted to retire.

I also wanted to be a good role model for my kids, help my mom and mother-in-law as they got older, and live my life free from owing anyone money.

With this exhaustive list of people and things that needed my attention, I had a lot of introspection to do.

My first step to keeping my money was to write down one immediate goal with a measurable timeframe.

The goal was to get out of debt within two years.

I went online and printed three months of bank statements for both my personal and business accounts to track my financial behavior.

It was not a surprise when I saw a pattern of swiping for dinners out and going to the movies every week.

Tony and I were spending at least $250 a week in those areas.

I saw these damaging spending habits and decided to take action. The more debt I paid, the more my anger turned into a straight financial beat down. I was dedicated and committed to knocking out this debt, and with Tony's help, it only took a year.

I equate my steps to getting out of debt to cooking. Much like when you are cooking, getting out of debt requires you to have different things going on simultaneously.

I love to cook. I have the power to make the food taste great or taste awful. This is just like debt. We have the power to do good with our money and pay our debt, or we can create more debt and ultimately be blinded by it.

Although I am about to present a correlation between kitchen burners and finances, this is a charting/spreadsheet method and is not meant to be taken literally.

You must approach the following exercise in a methodological sense, so you can understand that you must have multiple things going at the same time while you are trying to get out of debt.

So begins my cooking analogy or what I like to call

"the different burner syndrome."

When cooking, we have the option to turn the flame on low, medium, or high. When we cook on a high flame, we are usually boiling or frying food.

The higher the heat, the faster the results. This is where we place our debt, on the highest heat for the fastest results. We cook on a low flame with foods that need more time or those that need to be treated delicately.

Each saving component is going to be on low flame, for which you are taking your time building while paying off debt. Each burner is set up with an automatic draft or debit, which is deducted from your bank account as you see fit.

And remember, all four burners are working simultaneously.

BURNER #1 IS DEBT.

This burner is set on the highest flame.

You have a detailed plan to pay off your debt, and you are sticking to it no matter what.

You are aggressively paying off the smallest debt until the entire balance is paid in full. You will then apply this same momentum to the next debt and continue this process until all debt is paid.

This debt can be anything from credit cards to car loans to student loan debt. The amount you pay on this debt is determined by the remaining balance from paying for essentials such as mortgage/rent, food, clothes, and utilities. You are whippin this debt fast and hard. You decided to change your poor money habits and are ready to take control of your finances. There is no room for excuses on this high flame because you are burning debt quickly. You are tired of playing with your emotions and you are tired of thinking you will live the rest of your life in debt.

BURNER #2 IS EMERGENCY FUNDS.

Start building this account simultaneously while paying off debt by setting up an automatic draft out your checking account.

This transfer should be at least $100 each time you are paid. If you can afford more in this account, add it, but do not be aggressive in this area because you are stretching your money with a plan in other areas.

I would recommend no more than $200 a month for emergencies while you are still paying off your debt.

An emergency account is used for emergencies only, meaning something came up unexpectedly.

For example:

1) A loved one passes away, and you need to pay for travel expenses,

2) You lost your job and you need money to survive until you get a new job,

3) Your air conditioner stops working in the middle of August,

4) You or someone in your household becomes sick. An

emergency fund is not meant for an expensive purse, watch, or vacation. You want to make sure you have enough reserves for at least one month of expenses, such as rent, mortgage, utilities, and other expenses.

I recommend one month as a start because it is easier to calculate and obtain.

Once you have a month reserved, then work on another month of reserve until you have at least three months of emergency fund reserved. I want you to be as realistic as you possibly can.

If I ask you to reserve six months, that may be too difficult as you are starting off. After you are well developed in handling your finances, I do recommend having six months of reserve because it looks good and you will feel well accomplished.

Your emergency fund is calculated by adding your monthly household bills and multiplying the total amount by two or three months.

Based on your needs, the money in your emergency fund will cover the cost of your necessities when unexpected situations arise.

BURNER #3 IS CAR MAINTENANCE.

Anyone that drives understands that a car is an expense, like children. Your car needs fuel to run, oil changes every 3,000 miles, tires, breaks, and tune-ups to help protect the life of the car.

To this account, you will fund as little as $60 biweekly. It is not much, but the $60 adds up quickly.

Before we know it, we easily have enough money for an oil change without dipping into another area of the budget.

There is a catch to this burner. To prepare for the winter, beginning in September, I increase the car maintenance amount to $75 biweekly for all cold weather.

I can recall while we were on our journey using the burner method Tony called me one day after work in a panic, saying his tires were flat and he needed new tires immediately.

After listening to him say, *"How are we going to get me new tires so I can go to work?"*

I responded in a calm quiet tone, *"Come home, and get the car maintenance debit card; it will cover your tires."*

He said, *"What? We have the money?"*

I said, *"We sure do; we have been saving $120 a month in that account for about six months, you're good."*

He said, *"I am so happy I have a smart wife."*

Then is when Tony really understood that a person cannot have one account for everything; you must have an account with an attached debit card for things that will come up.

BURNER #4 IS TO PERSONALIZE.

Because we all have different areas that are important to us. I do not give this area a finite name.

This allows you the freedom to think about what you need to save for when the time comes.

This burner is entirely your choice based on what is important to you. This burner forces you to choose carefully and will force you to eliminate items that may not be important while you are changing your thoughts about money, which will force you to control your actions.

Christmas, Thanksgiving, holidays in general, birthdays, weddings, pet care.

This burner is for whatever area you think requires special focus.

The first three burners must be funded because they are your priority.

When I decided to stop getting whipped by debt and to start fighting back, it was October 2017, and the holidays were approaching.

I was not prepared; many of us are not.

We end up charging Holiday dinners and presents and slipping back into debt, having the mentality that we are going to pay off our holiday debt with our income tax check.

Once you pay off your debt, you will move your emergency account to the high flame burner where your debt was.

This took me a year to accomplish. It may take you two years or six months, just remember to keep up the pace and don't lose focus.

You must maintain the same behavior while building your emergency fund on steroids.

Remember when you are in debt, it is hard to save.

When you do not have debt, you can save and meet your two to three months emergency fund faster.

By moving your emergency fund to the high flame, you will

see your money grow faster.

After you have reached your emergency fund target amount, you can move your car maintenance and personalized accounts to the high flame and fund them however you see fit.

The good thing about the burner syndrome is you have a plan, and you control what burner you are going to fund most aggressively by choosing what is important to you.

This gives you full control of where you save and where you spend.

There is one final step involved in the Different Burner Syndrome.

Thus far, we used four burners, (1) debt, (2) emergency fund, (3) car maintenance, and (4) personal choice.

There is one area of the stove we have yet to account for, and that's the oven.

You need the oven to cook things slowly and evenly. For slow and steady savings plans, the oven will be used as your car account. I often hear my clients saying that their car has died or is about to die.

They agonize about how to pay for this without going further into debt by taking out an auto loan. The fact is that if you don't have a plan, you will get a car note because you need a car for transportation.

The solution is to plan ahead.

While your car is still working and getting you around, slowly build a car account.

Everyone that does not live in a major city where public transportation is easily accessed needs a reliable car. However, the truth of the matter is that not everyone may need a car. If you live in a city such as Philadelphia or New York, where you can take public transportation, this category can be used to save for another large purchase, such as a down payment for a house or a child's college fund.

If you do not have kids or a desire to purchase a home, then you can focus on the previous burners and build there.

The following is an example of how to build savings using your slow and steady oven account. This is how I did it, and it worked for me, so it can work for you as well.

For my car account, I was saving $285 a month.

This broke down to $142.50 biweekly toward a car for one year while I was whippin my debt.

I did this because, at the time, my 2007 Chrysler Aspen had over 180,000 miles on it. As I write this book, it's clocked over 225,000 miles and is still going strong.

I will not get rid of my truck unless Jesus himself taps me on the shoulder and says *"Okay, daughter, that is enough. You have done good things with the vehicle. You fed the homeless out of this truck for eight years, put the needy in your truck to minister to, and drove your son to Jackson State University in Mississippi. You can now let the truck rest in peace."*

Until that day, the Aspen lives. The oven method is a way for you to take your time and save for a decent car/home/college that will get you to where you need to be.

I am not going to give you an amount to save for because I did not have one. I knew I would not go overboard and save $10,000 or $15,000 for a vehicle. I was not going to purchase a car more than what I had in my savings account when I needed it.

That being said, it had always been my dream to own an old 1990's Lexus.

About five years ago, Tony was looking for a vehicle and came across a black and gold 1995 Lexus. I told Tony I wanted an all-cream or all-gold old Lexus with the sunroof, leather seats, and CD player.

I know a CD player is pretty much obsolete these days, but it's still what I wanted. One day, Tony sent me a picture, and there she was.

An all-gold 1997 Lexus, limited coach edition with cream-colored leather seats and a sunroof. The car only had 110,000 miles on it and was barely driven for over 15 years. I paid $3,500, and it was a no brainer. I had a little over that amount in my car account from saving it slowly using my oven method. That was the best and easiest car purchase I ever made because **I paid cash.**

If you do not take this same approach when it comes to a car purchase, you will rationalize going into debt over a costly item that loses value instantly when it is driven off the lot. I know this because I did the same thing three times in my life.

If I had a plan, instead of signing car notes, I could have been using that money to build my IRA or save toward the purchase of an additional rental property or our vacation home.

Track with me as I give true mathematical numbers and illustrate how my Chrysler Aspen drove me into debt because I was not prepared.

On February 6th, 2008, I financed a 2007 Chrysler Aspen with 41,000 miles that cost $25,007.25.

This means I had to take out a loan in the amount of $25,007.25.

After five years and 15.39% in monthly interest (what was I thinking???), I paid exactly $40,714.40 for my 2007 Aspen.

You heard me, $40,714.40 for a car that cost $25,007.25.

That is approximately $15,707.15 in interest.

I paid off the car, received the retail installment contract, and was sick.

This made no sense to me. I paid for a vehicle that cost more than I had in my bank account, or in my IRA.

I was literally driving around in my future retirement savings. From that point on, I decided no more car notes.

I would take my time, save slowly, and pay for my next vehicle using cash. My 1997 Lexus is proof that this method works.

The Different Burner Syndrome allowed me to be honest with myself. If I had chosen to focus on one savings at a time, I would have not been truthful to me. My life has so many different burners, a son in college, two kids going to college, and a teenager at home. This was in addition to anything Tony and I needed. Because my life had so much going on, I had to make a multifaceted plan that would work for my family and stick to it.

MONEY TIP:

Use a tracking or charting system in these areas to keep you focused and on track. If you want to learn more in-depth information on how to budget and pay your debt by using my free spreadsheet or need 101 financial coaching for a free consultation, visit wwww.stenellthemoneytherapist.com.

NINE

$THE BUDGET IS REAL/ENVELOPES, DON'T LEAVE HOME WITHOUT THEM (MY MOTHER'S PLAN)$

It is now time to outline your budget in detail. Thus far I have discussed financial communication styles and money habits, owning the word "no," and the value of extra income. In this chapter, you will learn how to aggressively pay debt while saving for your future along with the importance of having several bank accounts.

You will also learn that the most important tool to get out of and stay out of debt is changing the way you think about money and your budget.

Much of the way you see money comes from the way you were raised, at least that is true for me.

As they say, "The apple doesn't fall far from the tree."

My mom was my first encounter with budgeting money through the use of the envelope system.

When I was young, I recall watching my mom make a budget on the back of an empty bank envelope.

She would itemize her bills, total each bill, and get money orders for each item. With any remaining money, she would fill bank envelopes with cash to be used for gas, electricity, phone, food, and spending.

When we went to the grocery store, she would pull the calculator from her pocketbook and start calculating each item she put in the cart.

When we would get to the register, she would tell the cashier not to go over a certain amount, knowing what she had in her food envelope.

If the amount in the envelope was $150, my mom would ask the casher to tell her when she reached $125 so she would not go over the amount she budgeted.

As the total approached the $125 cutoff, my mom would start to put items back.

My mom would spend no more than the amount that was in the envelope. She did not carry credit cards and always had cash to buy food and make purchases.

When it was time to pay, my mom would pull an envelope out of her bosom. As a child, this was so embarrassing.

She would not hesitate to take the envelope out in front of whoever was around. Her rationalization was that this was the safest place for her money to be.

She would say, "Your envelopes will tell you how much you can spend." She would track the purchases she made by writing down what she bought on the envelope, so when the envelope was emptying, she would know what she purchased.

This is how I learned to budget for items that were not housing or utility related. This includes purchases of food, entertainment, haircuts, and other small luxuries. Using envelopes or itemizing the money in your wallet allows you to stay on track with your spending. It also allows you to save for big items such as furniture or appliances, so you will not have to charge it to a credit card.

My mom still uses the envelope system and itemizes every bill she pays at her tender age of 76. It is her lifelong money plan.

Without a road map, directions, or GPS, you would not be able to travel to an unknown destination without getting lost. It is much the same with managing your money. At this point, it should be clear that without a money plan, you will get lost trying to get out of debt.

If you do not have a detailed budget that works for you, you will have no idea where you are spending your money.

As Warren Buffett says, "Do not save what is left after spending, instead spend what is left after saving." He's a billionaire; he should know.

Without a budget, we cannot see what is coming in and going out, which results in the mismanagement of your finances. You cannot become wealthy if you do not see what you are doing with your money.

If there is no budget, there is no realistic plan. Let me break down the mindset of many of us. It is not that you are not responsible with taking care of your family, going to work, and paying bills.

The problem lies in a world that tells us, even urges us to buy, buy, buy, whatever the cost. Without you knowing, you get accustomed to an economic system in which you work hard to earn money, buy what you want, get loans, spend what you want, and when all else fails, charge it or get a second loan on your home and consolidate your bills.

This way does not work because you are putting a bandage on the wound and not treating the wound so it can heal.

There are two very important steps that must happen with your money before you pay for anything.

Step 1—commit to the budget.

Step 2—execute the budget.

You first must commit to the budget and hold yourself accountable. You are making an agreement with yourself to improve your financial condition.

It should be simple enough because you commit to everyone else, your spouse, your children, your job, your pastor, your credit card, your car payments, your mortgage, or rent.

Commitment is what we do, and sometimes we do not realize that we are putting everyone before us, so why not do something for yourself that will turn your finances around?

This commitment is very critical and putting it off will only make things worse.

The second step is to execute the budge before you pay anything. If your check is the same amount each time you are paid, then you want to have your budget planned out two or three days in advance, so there are no last-minute excuses.

We all know the feeling of payday. We are either happy that we have money or sad that we are about to pay bills. Whatever the case, you rationalize with yourself who you are going to rob, Peter or Paul. When in reality, you are robbing yourself if you do not have a budget.

Before you pay for or purchase anything, you must first list the money coming in (revenue) and itemize the money going out (expenses).

The money that is left over goes into your envelopes. Now the budget is real because you now have a written plan that you will follow to pay your bills.

A budget is fairly simple. What follows are my steps to budgeting along with a detailed example of how I budget each time money comes in.

To begin your budget commitment, you must follow these steps:

» **Go to the bank and take out only the money you need to fill your envelopes and pay bills, if you pay bills in person.**

» **If you pay bills online or call to pay bills through your bank, open an account specifically for bills and transfer the amount of your bills from your main checking account to your bill account. By doing this, you are not giving creditors access to your main checking account, and you have control over what you put in the bill account.**

» **Always leave a buffer of $25 to $35 in your primary checking account for monthly bank fees to avoid over-**

draft fees.

Each time you get paid whether it is weekly, biweekly, or monthly, you should have a detailed budget.

To start executing your budget, first list your income (revenue) for both spouses.

In the illustration below, the fictitious couple is paid biweekly in the same pay period. In my example, the couple is married and their money is in a shared account.

After establishing your income minus money allocated to your different burners, you will list the expenses to be paid in order of importance such as rent, mortgage, and electricity bills.

This list should also include any current debt such as car loans, credit card balances, and student loans.

The budget shows a monthly total revenue of $4,550 for this pay period minus a recurring debit of $405.

This is automatically deducted from their checks and goes directly into the designated low flame burner areas for emergencies, car maintenance, their personal choice of savings area, and car savings.

The recurring account is a long-term savings account attached to your main checking account

This leaves $4,145 for expenses and to fill their envelopes.

Their expenses total $2,382.

Their envelopes total $745.

The envelopes are items they will need immediately in that pay period, outside of bills such as offerings, school supplies, and gifts for a baby shower or a wedding.

This leaves $1,018 remaining to be applied to their smallest **debt** amount on the high flame burner.

THE BUDGET

Mr. and Mrs. paychecks = $4,550 (income)

EXPENSES	BURNERS (AUTOMATIC DEDUCTIONS)	ENVELOPES
Mortgage: $1,015	Emergency: $110	Tithes/offerings: $250
Life Insurance: $112	Car maintenance: $55	Food/groceries: $200
Cell phone: $140	Personalize (Holidays): $60	Mr. spending: $75
Water/sewer: $125	Car savings: $180	Mrs. spending: $75
Car payment 1: $280		Kids' spending: $20
Car payment 2: $225		Takeout: $20
Credit card: $135		Gifts Birthday/wedding/graduation: $30
Student loan: $350		Miscellaneous: $75
TOTAL: $2,382	TOTAL: $405	TOTAL: $745
		BUDGET TOTAL $3,532

Any remaining income, in this case the $1,018 goes to pay off debt on the high flame burner.

A Note for Businesses Owners

For those of you that have businesses or are starting a business, I have four accounts that keep me organized: Operating Funds, Merchants, Taxes, and Emergency.

I do not keep all business revenue in one account. I further explain each account in more detail and their functions on my podcast No More Excuses. Wake Up!

www.stenellthemoneytherapist.com/podcast

SPECIAL CIRCUMSTANCES

In some cases, you may have surplus money in addition to your paycheck, such as child support, social security, unemployment and survivors' benefits.

I did not forget about you.

I understand that you want to know what you do with this income because it is not listed in the above budget. In my case, I was receiving child support for my three children.

Once I got serious and, on a budget, I did not use their money to pay bills.

Instead, I put a portion of the child support toward college and also paid for their monthly expenses such as clothes, food, and toiletries.

I admit, I used to spend this money on bills, or anything for which I needed extra money.

But child support is intended for the child and should be used for the child. Don't forget, paying a water bill that keeps clean, running water available to the child does count.

As parents, it is our duty to make sure that we have a plan

for our children. If we invest child support money into a 529 college savings plan, it will help our children in the future.

Ultimately, it will also save you a lot of money by avoiding college loans and the frustration that is associated with college planning.

If you are on a fixed income and receive Social Security, that counts as revenue, and you will use that in the income section of your budget.

This is an area that you do not hear anyone talk about in budgeting because it may not be something they experienced or can relate to. I am speaking from experience, knowledge, and maturity.

My daughter Unique's father passed away when she was six years old. Her father also had an older son, so Unique's survivor's benefits were split in half.

It wasn't much money, but it was enough to put some away in a 529 college savings plan and helped with taking care of her needs.

After her father's passing, it took me four years to get it together mentally and financially.

I had to be direct with myself to understand my daughter's need for a college fund.

I was able to save over $10,000 using the survivor's benefits, which only pays for half a semester at most universities. Regardless, I made a choice to do right by my daughter. Once she turned 18, it was over, and I felt a sense of accomplishment.

Parents, if you are in any of these categories, I feel your

pain.

The experience is real; however, it is your duty to make sure your extra income is used to truly benefit your child.

There is also the assurance that you will never question where all that money went.

MONEY TIP:

Go to my website www.stenellthemoneytherapist.com to download my free budgeting spreadsheet with a built-in envelopes and special circumstances section. It will help you stay on track.

TEN

$THAT DAMN SALLIE MAE$

I instantly get a headache when I hear how much student loan debt undergraduates accumulate in their freshman year of college. As students struggle to maintain good grades to stay on track to graduate, those who took out loans will be required to start paying back thousands of dollars in just a few months.

Depending on whether the college is public, private, in or out of state, the estimated four-year cost of student loans can range from $40,000 to $139,000.

And here's the kicker, merely going to college does not guarantee you will make any financial return on your four-year investment. Still, college does equip you with the skills to hopefully land the career you want.

At any rate, you cannot expect anyone to give you information on how to pay for college. You must do the research and find out what is the best avenue to continue your education while not going broke paying back Sallie for the rest of your life.

If you do take the loan route and end up owing Sallie, you must be aware of the consequences if you default on your student loans. Because student loans are federally funded, the government can seize your tax refund, garnish your wages, prevent you from borrowing any financial aid, or you can be sued.

The U.S. Federal Reserve Bank states Americans owe about $521 billion more in student loans than in credit card debt. This equates to an estimate of 45 million borrowers and 1.5 trillion people who owe student loan debt.

That means just about everyone you know has student loan debt. Whatever the case, whether you saved and have a college fund for your child, or you owe Sallie, college is an investment.

This decision should not be taken lightly and must be accompanied by a plan that will help you to not go broke.

Many 18-year-olds just graduating high school have an idea of what they want to study in college but do not have a concrete understanding that every course they choose costs money.

Any decision of adding or dropping a class costs money, changing major's costs money, books, tuition, travel, toiletries, just breathing costs money.

I learned through trial and error to not allow my children to dictate what college I would be spending my money on. Most students are not realistic when applying to colleges.

As parents, we allow them to dictate what school they will attend because it was the college they dreamed about, or sometimes (like I did) we push certain schools on our children.

We don't realize how much future financial trouble we are getting ourselves into.

Eighteen is a very young age to be accountable to understand the steep costs of higher education. Eighteen is especially young to be completely serious about such a massive investment. Sometimes, as parents, we find out our child was not invested in learning and had another agenda.

I have three children who are millennials. Zaquell, who is 25, is a graduate with his master's degree in social work.

Ryann is a college sophomore, and Unique is a college freshman.

My kids do not have any credit card or car loan debt. Zaquell was blessed to get a full track scholarship from Jackson State University in Mississippi.

He does, however have some student loan debt from his master's program. Tony and I decided to gift our children their undergraduate education, so they would not end up with four years of student loan debt.

But we agreed not to pay for continuing studies.

Our children will have to pay and work for their higher degree on their own.

You may say they have it good because their mom is the money therapist, and they will get to learn all the tools that will help them make healthy financial decisions.

True, I preach about the importance of having a financial plan and educate them on money and credit, but ultimately the decision is theirs.

What follows are some beneficial points to help you educate your children on the responsibility of paying for college. After the hard knocks of life and years of research, this is what I do and suggest to my clients.

» Do not take out student loans for your child or go into debt with Parent PLUS Loans. The average Parent PLUS Loan is $35,600. That $35,600 becomes your debt, not your child's. You are responsible to pay this loan back whether your child finishes school or not.

» Do not let your child take out student loans. Instead, discuss a plan for a two-year college that costs three times less than a four-year college.

» Start talking to your child about planning for college as early as eighth grade.

» Talk to your child's ninth grade counselor to sign them up for college courses to earn college credit while in high school.

» Have a conversation and be real with yourself. You are the parent. If your child does not have a scholarship and you did not save for their education, then there is nothing to discuss. Your child will have to go to a community college and work part-time to help pay for their education. The average student loan debt is $29,800. You don't want yourself or your child to have this kind of debt, which does not include the car or credit card debt I am trying to talk you out of.

» Public colleges and universities offer a bigger bang for your buck. Public colleges are funded by the state government and therefore can offer lower tuition. The cost of private colleges is higher because they are funded through tuition and donations and owned by private organizations. Choose wisely.

MONEY TIP:

You can plan to have your child attend community college for two years and obtain an associate degree. These credits can then transfer to an in-state four-year public college. Tuition will be lower than an out-of-state college because you as the parent pay state income taxes.

ELEVEN

$CREDIT$

I had to really think about how I was going to write this chapter because discussing credit can be controversial depending where we are in our personal lives. I do not want to push my values regarding my personal feelings on credit, although I will share with you how I feel about credit card debt.

To fully understand the gravity of credit card debt, it is important to first understand the history and concept of credit.

A brief history of credit and credit reporting:

» **Derived from the ancient Mesopotamian Sumerian civilization in 3500 BC. Used throughout the ages of Babylon and the Roman Republic for the purpose of agriculture loans for grain and silver to farmers purchasing land.**

» **1803: The earliest account of credit reporting among English tailors who verbally reported to each other** when customers failed to pay their debts.

» 826: English tailors chronicled customers who failed to settle their debt through reports in a monthly newsletter.

» 1864: New York City's R.G. Dun & Co. created an alphanumeric system for companies who were creditworthy.

» 1899: The retail credit company known today as Equifax begins the compilation of creditworthy customers.

» 1919: After the introduction of Henry Ford's Model T (Tin Lizzie) in 1908, General Motors comes up with an installment financing plan since most families could not afford to purchase vehicles with cash.

» 1930: General Electric began to offer appliances such as washing machines and refrigerators on installment plans. Also, two out of three cars were purchased on installment plans.

» 1946: The Charge-It program was invented by John Biggins as the first credit plan between bank customers and local merchants.

» **1950: The Diners Club credit card was introduced.**

» **1989: FICO debuted as the first universal measurement of personal credit scores.**

» **1995: Consumer credit is reported regarding housing, employment, and insurance.**

As you can see, credit began with the purpose of purchasing land. It turned into purchasing cars on credit, then appliances, and ultimately led to the creation of credit cards.

Banks saw how they could capitalize on merchants and customer loans. Because of this realization, now the average American household's credit debt is $5,700.

Households with a weak financial strength, meaning a low net worth, hold an average of $10,308 in credit card debt.

Not to mention the $3.9 trillion in outstanding consumer debt and $1.03 trillion in revolving debt.

Looking at the numbers, we see the mindset of "buy now, pay later" has taken over the average household.

The leading mentality is that you must establish credit to apply for loans for expensive items such as a car or home in the absence of enough cash.

There is an alternate way of thinking that says no to debt and yes to budgeting to track where money is going. This mindset champions saving and paying cash for all purchases.

This split is evident even in the youngest members of the American workforce. There is a community of millennials that is embracing this new debt freedom wave and have decided not to go into debt.

These young people refuse to take out student loans and have learned how to survive with a budget, a plan, and save for their wants and needs.

On the other hand, you have a group of millennials who do what I did, finance cars they cannot afford, apply for credit cards and student loans, and live off refund checks that have to be paid back with interest.

By the time I was 20 years old, I owed over $6,000 in credit card debt, and my student loan debt was growing.

One has to wonder: What is going on?

Do we really need credit to help us obtain our needs and wants?

All these questions came pouring in my head as I taught financial classes and counseled clients to help them come up with long-term solutions tailored to how they see money.

Clients meet with me to seek guidance and advice to unlearn unproductive financial habits and to develop a plan that will help them be successful.

Their slate is not blank (Tabula Rasa, as we say in psychology), and they are coming in after their debt has become too much to handle and they have reached their breaking point.

However, young millennials have no credit and a blank slate. If they are taught the fundamentals of credit correctly, its pros and cons, and its purpose, they will learn productive behavior regarding how they approach and manage their credit.

I realize that most people cannot make cash purchases and need to use credit cards.

You may have a $2,000 open line on a credit card and, if used irresponsibly, will create a habit of spending more than you can afford to pay back.

When you do not have a blueprint, you don't know how much money you really have.

When you charge an item that you did not budget for, you are spending money that, in reality, you do not have. You may be approved for a high credit line of $11,000.

That does not mean you can afford to charge that full amount. It means you now have an $11,000 loan, and if you are not careful to pay the balance in full each month, you can get yourself into trouble.

Banks consider your eligible credit limit based on how well you pay your debt. You may be able to manage a $2,000 credit limit. However, an $11,000 credit line (while enticing for re-modeling your kitchen or bathroom) may not be manageable to pay.

This begs the question: *HOW CAN YOU BE RESPONSIBLE WITH CREDIT?*

To understand the answer, if in fact you choose to use credit, it is important to understand the fundamentals of credit and the purpose of a FICO score.

» **A FICO score is a predictive analytic measure used to examine consumer behavior to see if they will pay** their bills on time and the credit limit one can handle.

» Your credit score only exists because you borrowed money and you owe that money back. If you don't borrow money, you will not have a credit score.

» Credit score also indicates how good (timely) you are at paying back your debts.

» Credit score is not based on your income.

» Credit score is not based on how much money you have in your checking or savings account.

» A high credit score does not mean you are not struggling to pay your debt. It means you are paying your debt on time, so you appear responsible at paying money back to lenders.

» If you pay your debt on time, you have good credit. If you miss or make late payments, you have bad credit.

Nuggets of Wisdom for Millennials

I have reached a time in my life that I have learned to not live with debt other than investment properties and my home, which is listed as a goal to pay off in my financial treatment plan.

Yet, I cannot push my financial decisions on you. My goal is to educate and provide you with information, so that 20 years from now, you are not trying to pull yourself out of the pit.

As you know by now, I think consumer debt is bondage and does not allow you to live freely. However, there are many people that are responsible with paying consumer debt, and it works for them.

Now you need to figure out your approach, be wise, be responsible, and have a plan. Just because I get headaches thinking about paying back loans every 30 days, that doesn't mean you can't come to a different conclusion on your own.

As a therapist, my job is to leave you with some information to help you learn more and develop a plan that will work for you.

Here are some alternatives to traditional credit that may keep you from falling prey to debt.

» **Manual underwriting** is a process that evaluates your ability to repay a loan based on your bank statements and pay stubs. This method is different from the traditional automated process because it considers your financial ability to repay the loan rather than just meeting specific criteria such as a certain credit score and debt-to-income ratio. With this process, a human underwriter manually endorses the loan as opposed to an automated process that evaluates your ability to repay the loan, by verifying rental history through cancelled checks or alternative credit such as phone, cable water bill, or some combination of all of the above.

» **Secured credit** uses an initial deposit in the bank to open an account, which is why the cards are available regardless if you have established credit or not. Because you often cannot get a credit card without good credit, a secured credit card can help you build credit or correct bad credit. The secured credit card is backed using your own money so that you are in control of what you spend. This is in direct opposition to an unsecured credit card that is a loan and not backed by your own money. Secured credit cards can be used wherever credit cards are accepted, including online. I suggest that you use a secured credit card for making gas purchases and pay the balance in full each month. This will help you to not overindulge. You can set up automatic payments each month directly out of this account; however, you will be responsible to budget that amount in your biweekly or monthly budget. This will help build your credit history without applying for a traditional credit card and keep you from spending money you do not have.

Once your credit is established, you may want to use traditional credit cards; that is your choice.

I suggest you continue to use secure credit cards for producing passive income.

Passive income is income that you are not physically laboring to produce, such as real estate investments with rental income, or other business ventures in which you are not actively involved such as partnerships, enterprises, or for-profit business such as my case management agency that took me four years to grow.

The goal of a high credit score is to obtain a history of borrowing money and repaying loans. The debt free lifestyle is a choice that people make to simplify their spending and to avoid costly interest payments.

With this lifestyle, your credit will be non-existent, which is not necessarily good or bad. Ultimately, the choice is yours.

MONEY TIP:

Having someone pay you every 30 days is an investment. If you decide to use credit to produce passive income, real estate properties can be very profitable. Rental properties can help you quickly pay off the home and turn future rent payments into profit. While investments of this nature do come with a certain amount of risk, the venture is often worthwhile in the long run.

TWELVE

$THE GAME PLAN (YOUR INTROSPECTION)$

You did not pick up this book just for something to read. You picked up this book because you want to get rid of your debt once and for all. As you can see, to whip my debt, I did a lot of praying, failing, and acts of faith.

Here's the real secret: you can do it too.

Go for it.

Make the decision to do something different so you can get different results.

Believe in yourself because you are the only person that can make this happen. Below is a summary of how to mentally, financially, and physically prepare yourself to change your life.

These points will help you to conduct your own introspection and make changes.

This will be your blueprint, your checklist to assure you are on track to **WHIPPIN YOUR DEBT'S ASS!**

> **Think about the importance of your money and what changes you should immediately make to your spending habits;**

» Write down what happened to you financially to bring you to your breaking point;

» Identify your financial communication style and give it a positive tweak so that you can see the results in how you spend your money;

» Say no to yourself and others who are interfering with your financial goals;

» Get a part-time job, or work overtime, and apply all that money to your debt;

» Debt, emergency, car maintenance, personal choice, and your car account are all being targeted at the same time;

» Name each account to pay your bills and set up an automatic draft. Pay your bills from an account titled bills, so you are not paying your bills from your main checking account. This will help to avoid overdraft fees and creditors automatically taking money out your main account;

» Work out a plan to pay for college so you do not regret your decisions 20 years later;

» Prepare your budget the week you get paid to track

your incoming revenue and outgoing expenses;

» Fill spending envelopes aligned with the budget;

» The decision to live with or without credit is up to you and your definition of financial freedom; do your homework;

» Ensure that you and your spouse or partner agree with your financial plan.

THIRTEEN

$MY REALIZATION$

In my time working to help free others from debt, I have found that success in erasing debt takes ownership and an open mind along with a detailed plan.

It is hard work, but the hard work is worth the challenge.

Budgeting, a financial plan, the burner syndrome; they all work if you work it.

The feeling of being debt free is a feeling of happiness and autonomy because you are able to plan and spend money the way you want to spend it.

This is the freedom of not being held captive by your debt, your key to peace of mind.

Dare to be different and **WHIP THAT ASS, DEBT'S ASS THAT IS!**

www.stenellthemoneytherapist.com

About the Author:

The Change Catalyst: Stenell Greene-Myers

Multidisciplinary Leader. Survivor. Educator. Author. Advocate. Socialpreneur. Counselor. Financial Coach. Podcast Host. Speaker.

Stenell Greene-Myers is a multidisciplinary thought leader and advocate whose superpower lies in her undying commitment, tenacity, and vision to help individuals, families, and entrepreneurs pinpoint their strengths, combining them with hard work and creating CHANGE.

The Survivor . . . Raised in Camden, New Jersey, by a single mother, Stenell later became a teenage mother of three children, and subsequently a survivor of domestic violence and divorce. Her young life was epitomized by her search for love in all the wrong places. Still, she decided to reject the stigmas often associated with at-risk single mothers living in the inner city, envisioning it rather as her greatest strength.

The Educator . . . Committed to higher education, Stenell

has a master's in mental health counseling. As an educator for three years, she taught at Drexel University in the Behavioral Healthcare Counseling Department, as well as various psychology and addiction counseling and training courses at Camden County College. Stenell utilizes her expertise in mental health, behavioral psychology, and developmental disabilities to teach and train educators in schools, colleges, churches, employment offices, rehabilitation units, and prisons.

The Author... Stenell combined her passion for entrepreneurship and building healthy, rewarding relationships to author Who's Gonna Pay the Mortgage? A Woman's Guide to Relationship Recovery in 2010. She completed a new publication titled Whippin Debt's Ass! Stenell is also the creator of I-Female magazine, designed to inspire, motivate, and empower all women.

The Advocate . . . In 2012, in association with Trudean Haye and Canvas Hair Salon, Stenell worked to devise the I Am a Survivor Gala, honoring women who have overcome seemingly insurmountable life challenges.

Likely her most significant testament to helping youth and adults overcome financial, social, emotional, and academic obstacles was the creation of JOY (Just Our Youth: Making a Difference) in 2015. JOY is a current non-profit 501c3 afterschool youth academic enrichment program striving to help families break the generational cycle of poverty through educational and career achievement.

The Socialpreneur... In the same year, Stenell also founded A Second Touch, a Support Coordination New Jersey Division of Developmental Disabilities (DDD) funded service that currently assists individuals in gaining access to needed programs, state plan services, as well as medical, social, and educational services.

In 2020, Stenell added Direct Support Professionals (DSP) to A Second Touch, providing assistance and support to physically and intellectually disabled adults in daily living activities in the home and community.

The Counselor . . . Stenell's love for counseling drove her to establish and operate A Better Me Incorporated from 2017 to 2021. Partnering with the New Jersey Children's System of Care (CSOC), a division of the Department of Children and Families, the program provided an array of integrated and trauma-informed supports and services to youth with behavioral health challenges, intellectual and developmental disabilities, and/or substance use needs.

The Financial Coach . . . After paying off $50,000 in debt and becoming debt-free in 11 months, Stenell switched gears, reinventing her passion of helping people. Stenell lives by her personal motto: "If your personal finances are not in order, your business finances will not be in order." As such, Stenell became a financial coach by way of Dave Ramsey's Financial Coach Master Training.

Her training and expertise also led her to launch Money Therapy Institute in 2018, a 1–1 remote coaching program with the central mission to help families get out of debt and overcome poverty.

Stenell developed a financial spreadsheet treatment and behavior plan tailored to her clients' needs which educates, counsels, and coaches individuals and couples to successfully budget and become debt-free. This philosophy also extends to existing business owners and start-up businesses looking to develop a business treatment plan to project financial success.

Podcast Host... Stenell wanted to create an avenue for her to share on her own terms about finances, relationships, and mental health. She wanted to recreate I-Female magazine she released in 2010 in the form of radio. In 2020, Stenell launched No More Excuses. Wake Up! podcast where she interviews and talks about money, entrepreneurship, and life-skills that were not taught.

The Speaker... Today Stenell uses her story of empowerment to encourage teens to overcome barriers similar to those she has overcome. She is a sought-after speaker who educates and trains youth and adults in true entrepreneurship and debt freedom.

IN MEMORY OF MUHAMAD ALI (CASSIUS MARCELLUS CLAY JR.).

He taught me how to conquer my Goliath (finances) and never be afraid to be me!

YOU ARE THE GREATEST